Shades Of A Broken Heart

a poetry book

by

Cyndi Buchanan

Thoughts at 2 A.M.

Shades Of A Broken Heart
© 2025 Cynthia "Cyndi" Helen Buchanan

ISBN: 979-8-9920442-0-1

To my parents, Raymond and Myrtle, whose unwavering love and support have shaped who I am. To my brother, Raymond (Ray), who has always been there over the years to support me in anything I do. To my children, Melissa and Jim, for always being by my side.

To all the broken-hearted, who find strength in their struggles, and to the wonderful supporters and followers of my Facebook page, *Thoughts at 2 A.M.*, whose encouragement means the world to me.

With all my love,

Cyndi Buchanan

Photography by David Steiner

About The Author

Cynthia "Cyndi" Buchanan is a poet and former nurse who spent 50 years caring for others before turning her focus to the healing power of words. She has written poetry since she was a young girl, using her pen as a way to process life's joys and sorrows. Her work reflects the depth of emotion and resilience that has shaped her personal and professional journey.

Cyndi is the founder of a popular open mic poetry night in her hometown, where she encourages others to find their voice. She is also the creator of the Facebook page *Thoughts at 2 A.M.*, which has garnered a following of over 55,000, where she shares her poetry and reflections with an engaged and supportive community.

When she's not writing, Cyndi enjoys the company of her two beloved cats, Connor and Guinevere, and cherishes the time spent with her children, Jim and Melissa. In *Shades of a Broken Heart*, Cyndi invites readers to explore the complexities of love, loss, and healing, with poems that are as heartfelt as they are transformative.

About The Book

Shades of a Broken Heart is a poetry collection that tells the story of heartbreak, exploring the raw, often dark emotions that come with love lost. The poems capture deep sorrow, confusion, and vulnerability, journeying through the darker shades of grief and loss to the lighter, ever-enduring shades of hope and encouragement. The collection invites readers to confront their pain and forge a path forward, leaving them with a sense of resilience and the possibility of healing.

Table of Contents

And

So It

Begins...

AT WHAT COST

It's times like this
That I wish
Would never come
To an end

Remembering every nuance
Every touch
Of your fingertips

Every beat of my heart
At the touch of your hand

Every smile that I had
Right from the start
Owed to you
Oh, but at what cost

PIECE OF MY SOUL

My heart is shattered

It's broken in two

You now take

A piece of my soul with you

You were so much

A part of my life

Without you here

Brings an emptiness inside

I will recall

All the happy times

We shared

Thanks to my angels

For guiding me there

ENDLESS NIGHT

The time I spent with you

I felt so alive

Everything was always alright

We would laugh

Into the wee hours of the endless night

Your gifts to me

Were so thought out

I miss you so

You always held me so tight

But time moves on

And things change

Time to let go

Of what will never be again

But what will be remembered

Till my last breath

Or the strike of my pen

MAGICAL NIGHT

Oh, the memories

That come to mind

When I think of that magical place

Where we spent the night

Sweaty skin

Passion so intense

Heartbeats matching rhythm

With the fantasy in my head

Love

Like you've never known before

Heart bursting

Unable to catch your breath

Incense burning in the background

Rose petals strewn on the bed

The scent lingered on

Into the night

As you held me in your arms

Oh, so tight

Little did I know

That the end was in sight

And that silence

Could be so deafening

In the darkest of nights

YOU SAID

You told me

I was the prettiest of all

That I loved you

Like you had never

Been loved before

You would play me

Like songs on your guitar

We would dance in the rain

Spend hours talking and holding

Each other tight, till the morning light

Now I dance alone

As the tears flow

I told you that day

I would never be the same

If you walked away

And damn, you walked away

You just walked away

NO COMPROMISE

You felt the need to run like the wind

I felt the need to hold your hand

There was no compromise, no indecision

You took your aim, and shot me in my heart

With every intention to let me know that

We must part

Wow, that hurt

But you made me a Big Girl

Not needing anyone

Anymore

COME TO PASS

You only thought of yourself

Not of your actions that would come to pass

The ones that brought me, to my knees

Begging for mercy

This can't be

What's in store for me

Long lonely nights

With nothing to hold

As pieces of a broken heart

Start to unfold

But it's okay

I'll get by

I'm stronger

Than you ever imagined

Just don't look

Into my eyes

OWN IT

Who do you think you are

To waltz right in, and steal my heart away

Then steal away into the night

With my heart held captive

No ransom in sight

How could you do it

You knew what ghosting meant to me

Be a man and own it

Don't be a coward, and walk away

LOVE DIES

I just wanted to let you know

What your love meant to me

When I was yours

It was everything I'd ever dreamed of

What true love was all about

You showed me it was so easy

Or so it seemed somehow

But things changed as they sometimes do

And your love for me died

While my love for you grew, and grew

How do you let a love die

That is gasping for air

While you silently say goodbye

SEASONS

Times change just like the seasons

First you were mine

Now you're a stranger

How does that happen

From one extreme, to the other

It doesn't make sense, and it never will

That love can turn silent

As the pieces shatter to the ground

MERCY

Clouds up in the sky

Like the visions in my mind, move

With the fluid motion of the wind and time

And form pictures in my head that swim

And remind me of the times

When I was happy, love was real

This emptiness I now feel

Is like an anchor tied to my soul

My heart cries out for mercy

I can't take anymore

So much love to give

And nowhere to place it

I'll put it on a shelf

I don't want to waste it

LET ME GO BLIND

How could something so beautiful

Become so cold and distant

You know you're still the same

But their perception is different

You plead your case

To deaf ears

And you wallow

In your tears

If this is how it's meant to be

Let me go blind

So, I can't see

ALIVE

You made me feel so alive

So young, so vibrant

Like life wasn't gonna hurt anymore

Like I finally found my way home

Out of the dark and into the light

Like I'd never known

The day you said goodbye

The thought of it still makes me cry

It continues to break my heart in two

Why, oh why, do I still need you

The saddest part is

That you don't even know

How bad you destroyed me

You'll never know

I told you I'd be so devastated

I just couldn't even contemplate it

Now every day that goes by is a reminder

That I still stand alone

A Queen in an empty Castle

But stronger and wiser

With every passing year

Gone by

ONE DAY AT A TIME

There's nothing I can do
To change the way things are

You've moved on
And I have not

Broken pieces to pick up
And rearrange
To make some semblance
Of a life
Left in pain

One day at a time
The saying goes
I'll pick up the pieces
And move on

ABSENT

There is a song, that if it plays

The tears will flow, and I can't breathe

As I recall everything

How I felt every second

Of that night

How your memory, still holds me tight

Waiting for the day

When I will mend

And you will be

Absent from my heart and head

RIDE OR DIE

Music plays in the background

Pen in hand, tears released

Like a flowing river over the banks

Emotions finding words to describe

The hollow pain that I feel inside

At the death of what I thought was true love

Something that would never end

I thought you felt it too

I was your ride or die

Damn, you really made me cry

FOREVER LAY BROKEN

Why does it seem to be

That love promised

Sometimes ceases to be

It was everything that was good

And then you were misunderstood

How things changed overnight

And forever lay broken

With the ending in sight

You called on your angels

And your spirit guides as well

And you prayed to God above

To see you through

Strength was earned and so you stand strong

To face what life brings you by yourself

Head on

NEVER STOOD A CHANCE

Moonlight comes, the memories hit

I feel them right to my fingertips

I can actually feel you hold me

In a warm embrace

And plant a kiss upon my face

But that was then, and this is now

I don't even call you friend

It's like a love story

That never stood a chance

TIMES OF NEED

In times of need

You were always there

You always showed me

How much you cared

I could see it coming

Slow like a snail

Picking up pace

Intuition was my saving grace

Chose to remain blind

The thought of losing you

I would have lost my mind

Now that you're gone

I've got no choice

But to go on

And so, I did

Because I strive to be strong

When all hope is gone

BROKEN

Would it have made a difference

If I had told you before

That I was broken

Not the perfect person

I present to the world

There's no way to know

No way to change the past

It's time to move on now

And not second guess

LIFE MUST GO ON

If only you had loved me
Like I loved you
I wouldn't be in this place
Of grief and solitude

Nothing I said mattered
Your mind's made up
Our journey ends
And so, it goes

Life must go on
I know this to be true
Because the sun will rise tomorrow
And the moonlight will come too

The only difference is
I'll face them alone

You won't be standing by my side

As my refuge

But I am strong

I know this too and

With every day that passes

I'll be one more day over you

TIME AND TEARS

The wind blows

And I'm on my own

Once again

I never thought it would be possible

To ache so deep inside

That numb seems alive

Time and tears

Provide relief

Of pain so severe

You could suffocate, from the grief

To stand alone

Against the world

What a scary thought

For a shattered girl

So, one foot in front of the other

Day by day

Till strength is gained

And independence won

From the thoughts of two

Instead of one

EVERYONE SAYS

Everyone says

Just let it go

But how can you

When it has a padlock, on your soul

It was everything, that was good

Now it's nothing, but a broken heart

And memories, so beautiful

Now, too painful, to recall

STRONGER THAN THAT

When all hope is gone

Could you still carry on

The ache so deep, it draws your breath

From your chest

And puts you on your knees

Makes you wish you'd never seen

Those blue eyes or that smile

That took your heart away

It's like it never happened you ask

Did I dream it all

How long will these tears continue to fall

Until you realize you are stronger than that

Let nothing get in your path

Hang tough regardless, the circumstance

WITH TIME

I wish I knew, just when it was

That you fell out of love

Was it when, I was at my weakest

On bent knees

Tears rolling down my face

Screaming your name

I wish I knew

When the darkness, enveloped the flame

Because now, I will never be the same

Until I find some peace of mind

And that will come

With time

ETERNITY

When your love for me died
Why, oh why, didn't mine

Because you see
When I said I loved you
It was for all time, eternity

Not just when things were perfect
But when the tears left your eyes
I was there to provide comfort
Not listen to your lies

I stand now and look up to the sky
I will pray for the day
When this heart becomes whole
And the cracks in it, mended
And your memory

Long since gone

I will once again, stand strong

MISTAKE

As I lay here, I wonder

Why I even opened my heart

I knew this would happen right from the start

That wall that was so damn tall

I let the bricks fall but what a mistake

Again, my heart breaks

The warrior will once more stand tall

From the fallen ashes

She'll rise once more

BARE MY SOUL

I just want to know

If I'll be able to ever

Bare my soul again

Like I did with you

I saw what happened

It ripped me in two

I gave it all to you

And saved nothing for me

It ended abruptly

Or did it really

Was I just too blind to see

I have set you free

But I am trapped in a cage

One of my own design

In the center, a maze

That keeps me guessing

Which path to take

Cause there is only one exit

I can't afford to make a mistake

Time is of the essence

Life is over before we know

There is an urgency about it

I just must know

Please take my hand

And show me how

To let this all go

THE KEY

You might have left me

But your memory remains

You can't take that from me

I keep it locked away

Not because I want to

Because I'll be damned if I can find the key

That releases your memory

So, I can finally be free

MAGICAL

You made me feel unique

And special

One of a kind

It was magical

I think that is why

These memories won't die

And even though it's been years

The tears still flow

But that's okay

It doesn't make me weak

It made me stronger

Than I thought I could

Ever be

DEAD OF NIGHT

Sleep escapes me

In the dead of night

Memories of what

Could have been

Haunt my mind

I close my eyes

And there you are

Just like you were

The time before

For this won't end

You see

We'll meet up

In the next lifetime

Guaranteed

COME UNDONE

How do I let you go

Cause everywhere I look

Your memory is like a book

I can't put down

It haunts me and taunts me

Again, and again

Like a nightmare

You can't wake up from

All your feelings come undone

You scream for peace

But you find none there

The anguish you feel

Is more than you can bear

You swear there can be

No more tears to shed

As a new wave of lost emotions

Find their way in

Maybe one day

This pain will end

LOST

Just as time flows and can't be stopped

Nor can these memories

That continue to haunt

I've banished them from my thoughts

However, somehow, they manage

To just show up

So, I accept them and give them audience

One day I will release them

With deaf ears and blind eyes

Never to call them in again

They are lost for all time, in my mind

CLOUDS AND MEMORIES

As I sit and watch the Moon

Up in the sky

As the clouds and memories

Of us pass by

It conjures up what used to be

Then I open my eyes to reality

Of lonely nights

And a heart so broken

It will not mend

How many nights will I spend

Picking up pieces of self-worth

And rearranging them

So they don't hurt

It's okay, you'll be alright

Even in, the darkest night

THE THRONE

I was happy

The happiest I've ever known

You placed me high upon the throne

You placed the crown upon my head

You made me laugh

You drew me in

I believed in you

And all your lies

You thought you could fool me

With your disguise

But I saw right through it

Couldn't you see it in my eyes

CHAINED TO THE PAST

I can almost see it

That look in your eyes

When we were together,

And all was fine

Oh, but that was so long ago

Yet I linger here

Not quite ready to let go

With so much to lose

Only memories are left

That hold me here

Chained to the past

But with each passing day

I grow stronger in spirit

As your memory fades

And my journey becomes clearer

ESSENCE

If you only knew

How many times the thought of you

Crosses my mind

Your essence lingers

In my heart, soul, and mind

I think it will until the end of time

I want so much to release it

Because our love

Was never meant to be

One day I will walk away

From the memories

That still haunt me

UNDENIABLE STRENGTH

Do you ever think of me

Cause I can't make your memory

Less significant, you see

Why did you walk away

Our story wasn't complete

You left in the middle

Making me wonder

Why me

I continue to walk

This journey alone

Because no one

Can fill your shoes

I suffer on

But being alone

Brings undeniable strength

Because it's just you

To calm the wake

ETERNAL ACHE

I wish I knew

Just what it would take

To end this eternal ache

An ache that started long ago

To find the peace

I long to know

It started when you walked away

And continues on

With every passing day

I find the things that help me cope

And immerse myself in them

With all the hope

Of a Queen on her throne

On the throes of victory

As the war rages on

I will find peace

Within me

BEGUILED

Walking down the street at midnight
Trying to keep thoughts of you
Out of the bright Moonlight

For that's how I see you still
Alive in my mind's eye
Though it's been such a long time

Since you held me in your arms
And I was beguiled by your charms
And you said I was the one
Who had put the spell on you

That never happened
What you witnessed
Was true love, unconditional,
Raw emotion,

Twin Flame devotion

I wear the scar
Of that connection,
To this day
Of rejuvenation

While you just turned
And walked away
By doing that I thought
I would come unglued
But instead, I learned
To love anew

SIFTING THROUGH MEMORIES

That song comes on

And here we go

The roller coaster ride

Has just begun

Old memories haunt

The present it seems

No matter what I do

Tripping over the past

Becomes my only refuge

I need to find

Some peace of mind

And I know

That I will someday

But for now,

My healing involves

Sifting through

The memories of yesterday

And how I should

Have let you go

Before your silence

Struck its blow

DISTANT THUNDER

I close my eyes
To escape the pain
That crushes my soul
And drives me insane

How do I allow you
So much power
Over me
From thoughts and emotions
To my dreamtime fantasies

One day I will recover
And memories of you
Will be nothing more
Than distant thunder

WHEN I NEEDED YOU MOST

Where were you

When I needed you most

You weren't there

You were a ghost

Was it really that hard

To try to understand

That I wasn't perfect

What you had imagined

In your head

Yeah, you wrecked me

And that's a fact

But I came out stronger

And I thank you for that

Without all those tears I cried,

I never would have gotten

To the other side

The side where peace

And harmony reside

Regardless if you stand alone

Or in the company

Of another soul

DEEP THOUGHT

You sit in deep thought

In contemplation

Of all that's been lost

And you wonder why

The pain inside, just doesn't die

All you see

Are shades of gray and blue

It seems that

Everything is surrounded

In these hues

One day you'll find the key

To unlock the mystery

Of found love

To make beautiful memories

LOST SOUL

On this night, a cool breeze blows

The Moon shines bright

I need you so

You turned away

When I needed you most

To this day, my soul is lost

I, myself, one day I know

Though this journey is tough

I will show

The strength of a warrior

Banishing memories

That didn't want to go

I NEEDED YOU

The night breeze

Washes over my skin

And your memory invades

My thoughts again

It engulfs my soul

Making it hard to breathe

I needed you when

You needed to leave

If I only believed I was worthy

Of so much more

Than you ever could have given me

All I ever wanted and needed

Was Love

SAW IT COMING

Why do your pretty words

Echo through my mind

When spoken out loud

They become lies

What you said and what you did

Were totally opposite

I saw it coming

But did nothing

SIREN'S SONG

How will I ever learn

To let you go

You were everything to me

For so long

You were everything

I always wanted

Now, I'll always want

For what has gone

Change will come

When new love sets in

And old memories fade out

To a siren's song

Playing in my head

SAY GOODBYE

When do you start

To say goodbye

At the very beginning

When you saw

It wouldn't last

It didn't have the grace

What it took to surpass

The test of time

When they couldn't even

Look you in the eye

They knew they couldn't hold your gaze

Because you could read them

Like a magazine

If only they would have been honest

Your heart and soul

Might have found solace

Your spirit could have risen so high

And life was so beautiful and kind

Now at best

Sorrow is my friend

But my faith and hope

Chime in

To hold on tight

It's only a matter of time

GHOST

The beautiful sound of rain falling

On a bright sunny day

Hopeful it will wash away

This heartbreak

Waiting for the rainbow to take shape

To change my outlook of despair

To one of "I don't care"

You were not there

When I needed you most

You didn't care

You were a ghost

Go haunt someone else

And let me be

Your love is conditional

I set you free

BY CHANCE

In a love state of mind

Could I really have been that blind

To miss all the red flags

That were thrown at my feet

To be oblivious

Meant no defeat

But the silence was deafening

Emptiness all-encompassing

To release the pain

Tears flowed like rain

With each tear that fell

Strength ignited within my soul

I begged my heart

To just move on

Life is too short

To hold on to the past

Look forward to tomorrow

Good things happen by chance

EXPIRATION DATE

I'm so lonely I ache
This smile hurts to fake

The room echoes silence
The dim lighting seems vibrant

Recollection of time gone by
How it will never be again
In this lifetime

If I knew our love
Had an expiration date
I would have kept on walking
Make no mistake

QUITE CLEAR

Why did I need you so

If I had only wanted you

It would have been so easy

To let you go

Instead, I hold on

To some ancient memory

Where your words

Matched your actions

In my dream-like fantasy

I see now

What I couldn't see then

I was blind to the facts

Though they were laid out

Quite clear

I now love myself

Don't need anyone

To complete me

Took a while to get me there

But every baby step

Saved me

8 X 10

Can you feel the pain

When you realize

You will never be the same

What you thought was forever

Was just someone's moment

In time

And you wish that you never

Had felt so sublime

You wander now

With no known course

You could care less

If it's sunny, or if it pours

Get out of your subconscious

That vicious cycle repeats itself

Over and over again

Like an echo

Reverberating in your head

Staring at that 8 x 10 again

Won't bring you back

But it conjures up

Beautiful memories from the past

I try so hard to let go

You found that so easy

I struggle to carry on

It's just not fair

But life never is

I'll find someone else

When I find myself again

YOU'RE GONE

The waning gibbous Moon
Is in view
And all I can do
Is think of you

I look at photos from the past
And wish like hell
We had made it last

You walked away
So easily it seemed
Yet I hang on
Refusing to see reality

The facts are you are gone
It's time for me, to move on

MAYBE THEN

When I needed you so

Why did you have to go

As I stood alone

And wondered why

Again, I'd face

An empty sky

My soul so empty

My heart destroyed

My mind confused

For all time

Wondering if I'll ever recover

To love again

When your memory dies

Maybe then

SITUATION

As I look up in the sky
On this full Moon night
I'm so down and out
I can't find the light

I know it's there
I've seen it shine bright
But that is not
The situation tonight

A song came on
It took me back
To a time in my life
When you were mine
In fact

It was so long ago

But sometimes feels like yesterday

That these memories

Will haunt me

Throughout the day

I'm stronger now

Than I've ever been

The battle to maintain

The growth and not digress

Has me manifesting

A divine love, protected by

The angels above

AFTERGLOW

When I vanquish your memory

I will hold on

To the afterglow

Because right now

The memories invade me

Both night and day

They just won't let go

But the day will come

When the memories fade

And stop cascading

Down my face

On a new journey

I will begin

To live my life

Once again

No thoughts of the past

Holding me back

Dragging me down

This long dark tunnel

I now reside in

IN YOUR EYES

Why is it after all this time
I can still see that look
In your eyes

That look of intimacy and love
That spoke of a lifetime together
Of hope and magic to come

Somehow the spell was broken
My love fell
My heart lay broken
For all to see
As you turned
And left me

Lying on the ground
Screaming your name

Won't bring you back

Only causes me pain

I told you so

I'd never be the same

If you ever decided

To walk away

PRETENSE

Do you ever wonder why

You even try

It's like hitting a brick wall

Time after time

It makes no sense

To continue with the pretense

No matter how many times

You wish it would be different

It's always the same

The tears and the pain

They fall like rain

On a broken heart, that remains

WASN'T MEANT TO BE

You could spend your whole life

Holding on to someone

Who wasn't meant to be

You could tell from the very start

If he broke your heart

You'd never be the same

And so, he did

He broke your heart

And life goes on

But you have no spark

The embers now barren and cold

You felt so young and in love

Now you feel so alone and old

One day at a time

Is the best you can do

Don't look for love

It will find you

I SURRENDER

I surrender to the memory of you

Because what good does it do

To pretend it's not there

When I see and feel you everywhere

I wish it weren't true

It's all I can do

To get through the day without you

When the day finally comes

And I can no longer recall

What we had long ago

I'll have moved on

From the past, at long last

I'll remember

That the journey

Was long and hard

To get me there

But worth the tears and pain

At all the knowledge I gained

How to become just one

When society convinces us

That we need someone

SAME MISTAKE

It's only when you're all alone

That the memories

Invade your heart and soul

They make you feel such an ache

You'll never make

That same mistake

The mistake

That led you down the path

Of no return

You gave it your all

You stood so tall

Yet you still didn't get

What you wanted

And needed

Pick up that crown

It's easily found on the ground

Where you left it

SOMEONE

If only peace would come

When the night sky falls

And the day is done

It seems that's the time

When it's always worse

Those memories of us

Come to the forefront

I remember the good times

And how you made me laugh

But it sure doesn't

Make up for the time

My heart got crushed

I learned to pick up the pieces

All on my own

And grow stronger and wiser

With each day

No matter how long

I thank you

For what you taught me

To depend on myself

Not someone I thought

Was someone they're not

THE FOOL

That new Moon night

When I first looked into your eyes

And the excitement there

Couldn't be denied

Then you kissed my lips

Totally caught me by surprise

And the passion there

Couldn't be denied

Why in the world

Did you have to lie

You should have let me go

Much sooner than you did

You made me play the fool

I didn't deserve that

WONDERLAND

It's late at night
But sleep evades me
Flashbacks to a Wonderland
Full of love and excitement

Was it real or just imagined
Sometimes I think
It never happened

But I have memories
That tell me different
Your love felt real
I was coherent

Then I felt our love die
And my heart broke in two
And I knew in that moment

I'd grieve the loss of you

As each year passes

I still think of you

And wonder

What would have happened

If I'd never lost you

PROMISES WERE LIES

I pray for the day

I move on from this pain

I see it in my reflection

Feel it seep into my bones

Tears my only release

Emptiness, reverberates to my soul

How could you leave me

Your promises were nothing but lies

I believed every word

How I put you on a Throne

You threw me to the lions

No mercy was shown

I will rise

Make no mistake

My battle wounds are healing

Each and everyday

Thank you for the lessons learned

Scars worn proud

And bravery earned

RED FLAGS

I tried to quiet my mind

But my heart and soul

Won't be that kind

They are upset with me

For believing all the lies

All the different times

The red flags were present

I turned a blind eye

I just couldn't accept it

Now that it's over

I wish them the best

For this debacle

Will lead me to my destiny

What was meant to be

Will be

Fate has intervened

SHATTERED PIECES

I don't understand
How it came to be
That you could break my heart
So completely

All these years
There'd still be shattered pieces
On the ground
Far from where
They should be, by now

You broke my soul as well
I don't think
It will ever mend

I wish I knew
When the time would come

That I'd feel peace

Instead of numb

I'll bet it's when

I look within

To find the strength

I earned through ache

FULL REGALIA

How do I keep the night at bay

It's not so bad during the day

But when the night falls, I sit all alone

And I know that I can't even pick up the phone

What would I even say to you

You made it so clear,

When you said nothing, I feared

That sparked a fire from deep within

It raged from inside me

And the warrior became real

I won't be taken down this time

I'll stand like a Queen dressed in Full Regalia

Feeling sublime

RUN

When you only dwell on the good times

Of a relationship gone bad

You lose focus on the reality of what it was

That you actually had

He said he loved you

You wanted to believe it was true

When you realized he never really loved you

You just wanted him to

Who's at fault here

When your intuition was screaming to you

Turn and run it said

Yet

You chose to crash and burn

RETROSPECT

Above all else

I loved you well

But it just wasn't enough

To hold you close

In retrospect

It never was

You told me so

In so many words

I chose to be deaf and blind

To all the obvious signs

Laid all out in front of me

If I only would have chosen to see

What was right there

For all to see, except me

MEMORY OF YOU

As I sit and think

Of all the wasted time I spent

Going down memory lane

Getting lost in the fog

Of a beautiful love, gone so wrong

It keeps me from moving on

And starting my new life someday

I pray to God and the universe too

To help me forget

The memory of you

LIES AND DECEIT

Did you ever just need to cry

To release the tears

From so deep inside

Your soul cries out

For love and peace

But all you can find

Are lies and deceit

Yes, it hurts like hell

To be taken so low

But your climb back out

Made you much stronger

Than you know

YOUR MEMORY

Sitting here and wondering why

I can't seem to get you off my mind

Time has passed

The ache should be gone

But for some reason, it lingers on

I try and I try to carry on

So, I put a smile on my face

For all to see

When deep inside I cry endlessly

I pray for the day

When I can release your memory

UNENCUMBERED

The tropical night air

So thick, it's so hard to breathe

The tears running down my face

Blind me so I can't see

The only thing left

Are all these emotions I feel

And there's nothing deadening them

Hasn't been in years

I think I know the answer

To this puzzle that I live

But the piece remains missing

From the picture I created in my head

Every night as I slumber

I pray your essence returns to me

Unencumbered

SO DEEP

How did you get

So deep within my soul

I can't for the life of me

Just move on

I've tried every way

That I know how

Instead of getting easier

It's getting harder

Than anyone should have to know

I continue to pray

That the day will come

When I awake

The sun will shine

And my thoughts will be focused

On a new love this time

IN A BOX

The bittersweet memories

I have of you

Lay at my feet

In a box you will find them

Tucked away so neat

Behind the couch

So, no one can see

For me to bring out

When I'm feeling lonely

It doesn't do me any good

When will I learn

I'm the only one

Who is holding on to the past

That is long gone

EACH MEMORY

My soul felt lost

My heart lay shattered

For all to see

My mind recounted each memory

Every day the same

One just like the other

Putting one foot forward

In front of the other

But days turned to weeks

And months to years

Still your memory haunts me

Like you're still here

Things will change

When new love arrives

And my heart and soul will once again

Feel alive

ENOUGH

You wonder how the damage

Runs so deep

It was years ago

Yet it continues to seep

Into your thoughts

When you least expect it

That song comes on

You're back in time

You wish it was Déjà vu this time

Instead

It's a knife to your heart

Tears run down your cheeks

Another night without sleep

That day will come

I won't give up

When peace surrounds me

And my love is enough

FORGET ME

No, you won't forget me

Because I'm buried in the deep recesses

Of your mind

One of these days

Our memories will haunt you

They will make you catch your breath

And bring you back in time

INDIGO BLUE

Sitting here and wondering why

This pain I feel so deep inside

Where does it come from

I wish I knew

It washes over me

Like indigo blue

A lot of time has passed

I should be healed

Yet memories bring me back

To a happier time

When love was real

As the rain falls from the sky

The angels cry

They want me to be happy

And so do I

Letting go of the past
It's just so hard to do
Just depend on yourself
To see you through

HURT

Why does the hurt linger on
Long after the love has gone

The wound felt fresh
Even though it's a year since

I don't love you any longer
And the sting of betrayal
That took my breath away
Only served to make me stronger

REMEMBERING WHEN

It's only when it's quiet and still
That the memories surface
From deep within

You want so much to put them to rest
But what would you do
If they didn't haunt you so much

You could believe in yourself once again
That you didn't need the old memories
To remind you, when

You were happy and carefree
And you loved life everyday
And it didn't matter what was happening
You knew it would be okay

But staying in this place

Of grief and loss untold

Only stifles your spirit

Your heart, mind, and soul

Break free from the chains

That hold you bound

So, you can shine your light

To find your crown

THE DOOR

What do you do
When you're not sure
If you'll ever be able
To shut the door

The door that needs to close
So, another can open

With time they say
All things will heal
But this wound is too deep
And embedded, I feel
It might never close

Or my dreams come to fruition
But I'll keep trying to manifest
Positive intention

To surround me

And light the way

To guide me

So, peace and love

Can find me

NOT MY DESTINY

If only you had loved me

Like I loved you

Oh, how my life

Would have been different

Instead of lost

In the memory of you

Instead of feeling empty

My soul would have overflowed

With joy and happiness

Like I had never known

But that was not

Meant to be

You were not

My destiny

Am I meant

To walk this path alone

Sometimes I think

That is so

NO LONGER FRIENDS

Why is it now

When you're shown love

You run like the wind

What are you afraid of

Is it that time

They ripped your heart out

From your breast

And stomped on it

In silence they went

How all that was good, changed

Is beyond me

From lovers to strangers

No longer friends

Distance remains

Our journey ends

TIME AFTER TIME

Time after time

I let you back in

In hopes that you'll love me

Differently this time instead

It's always the same

When will you learn

Love is not a game

And I'm not your pawn

NOT WORTHY

I gave it my all

You gave what you could

I should have known then

To run like the wind

I can't believe

I ever gave you that much power

You were not worthy

I was destined for better

LETTING GO

Letting go
One of the hardest things
You'll ever know

The heart wants to hang on
But the soul knows
The essence is gone

The mind starts to replay
Every memory stored
From beginning to end
With everything in the middle
Thrown in

You see change
As an impossible task
When it's really easy

To stumble on the past

BROKEN PROMISES

You'll never understand
What you did to me
I now look at things
So differently

I thought I truly
Mattered to you
You hid it well
In disguise

Broken promises
Bold-faced lies

The day will come
When you'll be the one
Who's standing alone
And has no one

LIVE AND BREATHE

When the memories hit

It takes your breath away

Your eyes sting

The tears well up

You call out their name

But you know things

Will never be the same

You're afraid

Your heart has died

But you live and breathe

Just the same

Oh, but your soul did survive

But it is so lost and paralyzed

One more time

Your mind screams out

You've got this

Don't lose yourself

It's only a matter of time

Till you heal what's broken

And then, how you will shine

WORLD OF MISTRUST

Unconditional love

Unconditionally given

Right from the start

Magic, from the very beginning

There were comfortable, quiet times

And times when we were sad

And then there were belly laughs

From the jokes that we shared

Oh, how I miss what we had

That's for sure

But

Some love will die

Let go when you must

Don't let it keep you held prisoner

In a world of mistrust

RECLUSE

If I could just cut the cord

That holds my broken heart hostage

As it was, from the very start

Maybe, I could breathe again

And learn to love once more

Not be a recluse in the castle

That I built from pain

Sitting here driving myself insane

But venture out into this world again

I'll put a smile on my face

And be thankful

For all the beautiful things in life

I took for granted sometimes

I will know I am enough

Lessons learned

Now they're taught

I WONDER

I wonder when the day will come

When your memory is nothing more

Than a distant light, on a fading shore

I'll be unencumbered

By all those things

That keep me chained to the past

With all the beauty I've seen

But with that beauty

Came heartbreak so deep

That it took years to regain

My pride, you see

But now I stand taller

And stronger, and wiser by far

It will take a strong man to love me

For he must break down the wall

The wall that I built to protect

Not only my heart

But my soul

I know that he is out there

But I'm in no hurry

To find him

I'm loving who I am now

Took me years, to find her

SECOND CHANCE

As much as I loved you

And the memories still haunt

There's just no way

A second chance could be bought

The heart broken, beyond repair

I asked myself, how did he dare

Abuse a love

That was so precious and true

You walked away, when I needed you

The anguish you felt

Left you barren and empty

But with the tears that you cried

Came strength unending

The lesson learned here

Was oh, so clear

You can stand alone
In the face of fear

PASSAGE OF TIME

Just as the haze

Covers the moon tonight

The memories

Are now clouded

This can't be right

You could almost bring them

So vivid to mind

But the memories

Are now fading

With the passage of time

You should be relieved

To say the least

But the emptiness you feel

Brings no relief

It's like a bad habit

You know you should break

So, measure your happiness

By the strength

That you've gained

TEARS AND HEARTACHE

When you loved me

I had a smile

That could light up a room

When you left me

My smile faded

My heart felt empty

Filled with doom and gloom

As the time passes by

I realize we all must try

To not dwell on the past

It's a lesson learned

Regardless of the pain

You will endure

You'll come out stronger

On the other side

Of tears and heartache

When you trust

Your own guiding light

PURGATORY

It shouldn't matter anymore

Just shut the damn door

Forget what they appeared to be

Their actions spoke volumes

How long will it take you

To see

That you're meant

For so much more

Than this purgatory

That you endure

You don't need someone

To complete you

Find yourself

And life will create a path

Of joy and happiness

SILENT TREATMENT

Silent treatment

Was the method

To end the relationship

No words needed

They didn't have the courage

To say goodbye

It's at times like this

You wonder why

It meant so much

It made you cry

As the days turned to months

And months to years

You look at things differently

Now, without fear

Your pain

That once destroyed you

Has turned to gain

With confidence

Riding shotgun

Through your veins

MOVING ON

The raging fire

Has turned to ashes

They smolder

And then quietly die

A meaningful death

Lessons learned

Heartaches spent

Moving on

Is worth the pain

Because of all

The knowledge gained

It feels so good

To finally breathe

And know

You don't have to worry

About all eternity of yearning

For something that's not right

For you

Getting on with your life

Is what you should do

FINALLY FREE

Am I destined

To live this life alone

Sometimes I wonder

If this is so

And if that is the way

It is meant to be

I'll learn to release the memories

That hold my soul

Hostage and bound

So I can finally

Be free

To live a life unchained

From the ghost

Of your memory

FIT FOR A QUEEN

Every brick I dismantle

From this wall

I built around my heart

Mind and soul

I'm going to build a Castle

Fit for a Queen

Built of stone and mortar

And bright new shiny dreams

I thought the emotions

Broke me

Right down

To my soul

But I was mistaken

It made me whole

I've never felt more confident

And free

I thank you emotions

For the misery you caused me

You made me stronger

Than I ever thought I could be

I FORGIVE YOU

I forgive you

For hurting me so

It's the only way

I'll be able to let go

To let go of the past

And all that it meant

Will kill me inside

How do I make it

Not important

By loving myself

And all that I am

Will give me the strength

To stand up and command

What's meant for me

Will finally be

IF I LOST YOU

I used to believe

If I lost you

I would cease to breathe

Time would stand still

And my heart wouldn't beat

Well, I did lose you

But I gained myself, (me)

And it's really beautiful

When you find yourself

You finally become free

"US"

With tears in my eyes

Love in my heart

Emptiness in my soul

I release "US"

So I can become just one

To learn and grow

To find my light

To make what feels so wrong

Become what feels so right

I know it will…

In time

Acknowledgements

Kaileia Suvannamaccha, my dear friend and fellow poet, also known as The Princess Poetess, who played a major role in helping me through the independent publication process. Thank you, my Goddess, from the bottom of my heart, for the time and effort you devoted to helping me accomplish my goal and turn one of my biggest dreams into reality.

Melissa Zanetti and Jim Schaefer, my beloved children, my rocks, thank you for always being there and supporting me and all my dreams and aspirations. I love you both with all my heart.

Grace Crnojević, thank you for beginning this project with me. You were extremely helpful in getting set up with Ingram Spark, Bowker, and Amazon.

Kimberly Stanford, thank you for your unwavering love and support, always, and for being a moderator on my ever-growing Facebook page.

Erika Beddiges, my best friend in Pennsylvania, who has been there since I was six years old, we go beyond soul sisters. Thank you for all that you have done for me in accomplishing my dreams of becoming a published poet, professionally and personally.

Carolin Parent, my best friend in Florida, always listens to the new poems I write before I put them out. You have helped me as a collaborator on a poem, and I thank you for that.

Tina George, thank you my dear friend for accompanying me for my photos for this book. You were extremely helpful, and you calmed me with your relaxed demeanor. You have also always supported me long before Thoughts at 2 A.M. For that, I will love you always.

Patrick Britton, where do I begin? You are one in a million! You are always there to support me in any way you can, from making sure I get to my performances to helping me take care of my home, so I have more time for writing. I can never thank you enough.

Louisa Wargo, my beautiful Goddess and fellow poet, Lotus Rising, you are always there to support me and bring me little gifts to show your love. I appreciate you and love you more than you will ever know.

Marina Vongphachanh, an integral member of the Stardust Goddess Alliance and owner of Stardust Café, without you, there would be no

Open Mic Poetry Night. Thank you for opening your heart and doors to the poets in our community who desperately needed a safe stage to share their voices.

Terry (Tbone) Rhodes, thank you from the bottom of my heart for pairing music with poetry. With your skill and talent, and your amazing band, the Future Urban Zoo, my words take on a whole new level of meaning.

Frank (Bubba) Henson, you sir, are a poetic genius, and have been a valued mentor to me over the years. Thank you so much for introducing me to, and including me in, this vibrant poetry community.

Brian Baresich, you are a gifted and talented poet, and visual artist, and I am honored to call you, my friend. You have taught me how to become a better performing artist. Thank you.

John Gorski, a man who has owned my heart on more than one occasion, thank you for your unwavering support of my poetry by even sending me new beautiful journals.

Terrence (Terry) Wall, thank you for always being there for me and your continued support of my poetry, and my life in general.

Ron Brandt, thank you for always being there to support me as a dear friend. You go above and beyond always to help me with anything I ask of you. I appreciate it more than you will ever know.

Jayson Harper, at *My Salon Suites Suite 303*, thank you for your talent and artistry in hair and makeup, which made me feel beautiful in my first official author portrait.

David Steiner, from *Divergent Image*, thank you for making my first author photoshoot such a memorable experience. I love the portraits you took of me and will cherish them forever.

Finally, thank you to anyone who has broken my heart. You have made me realize that I only ever needed myself. Every shade of my broken heart only brought out the best in me, my poetry.